Imagining the Past at Mount Misery

Ron McAdow

PHP

Personal History Press
Lincoln, Massachusetts

About this Book

My intention is to share what I have learned about an unusually interesting place—a colonial-era sawmill site surrounded by dramatic ice-age topography—the Mount Misery Conservation Area in Lincoln, Massachusetts. Power for the mill was provided by Beaver Dam Brook, which flows through both ponds on the property.

I intend this publication to be useful in either the woods or the armchair. Visits to the described locations will make the text most meaningful, but because it is not possible for everyone to walk these trails, it is hoped that this material will also give pleasure to indoor readers.

To roll back the years, we use visual evidence that is still before us, and written information where it can be found. Since nobody was taking drone videos over Glacial Lake Sudbury, nor mobile phone pictures of the colonial sawmill, our time travel must occur in our imaginations. The images we conjure bear an unknown relation to the former reality—but they are what we have. The process of forming such pictures from scattered bits of knowledge has the fun of a jigsaw puzzle and the allure of peering back through centuries.

Prehistory

No doubt prehistoric natives hunted and gathered food around Beaver Dam Brook, but to judge by logic and the yield of artifacts, the fertile land west of the Sudbury River (formerly the bottom Glacial Lake Sudbury) was used more intensively than sandy, stony, Mount Misery—just as it is today. Lacking information about indigenous peoples' occupation and activities in the area immediately around the brook and hill featured here, our interpretation begins with the colonists, after acknowledging—with a shudder—the disaster that European diseases and displacement brought to the natives of the contact period.

A Concord farmer found this projectile point in a field near the Sudbury River.

Historical Background

English Puritans began colonizing Massachusetts at Cape Ann in the 1620s. In 1629, some of them moved from Salem to Charlestown. The next year, as their numbers began to swell with the decade of the Great Migration, two new towns were founded at the mouth of the Charles River: Boston and Watertown. Boston was a peninsula—three hills surrounded by water. Watertown, located where the Charles falls into its tidal estuary, extended to the west, and included present day Waltham and Weston.

Massachusetts winters were longer than those back home; New England farmers needed a lot of hay for their cattle. As the population increased, the demand for hay exceeded the supply from salt marshes. River meadows ten miles west of Watertown drew attention, then settlers. In 1635, Concord became the first inland town, followed in 1639 by Sudbury. Both towns had large riverside grassy meadows; the natives called the area Musketaquid in reference to that grass. Like Watertown, the original boundaries of Concord included land that later broke off into separate towns.

Land transportation was by trails that became cart paths. If they led somewhere many people wanted to go, paths became town ways, and were maintained by the community. Carts pulled by oxen were the principal means of moving goods over land; the best route for a road had the fewest and gentlest gradients and stream crossings, and

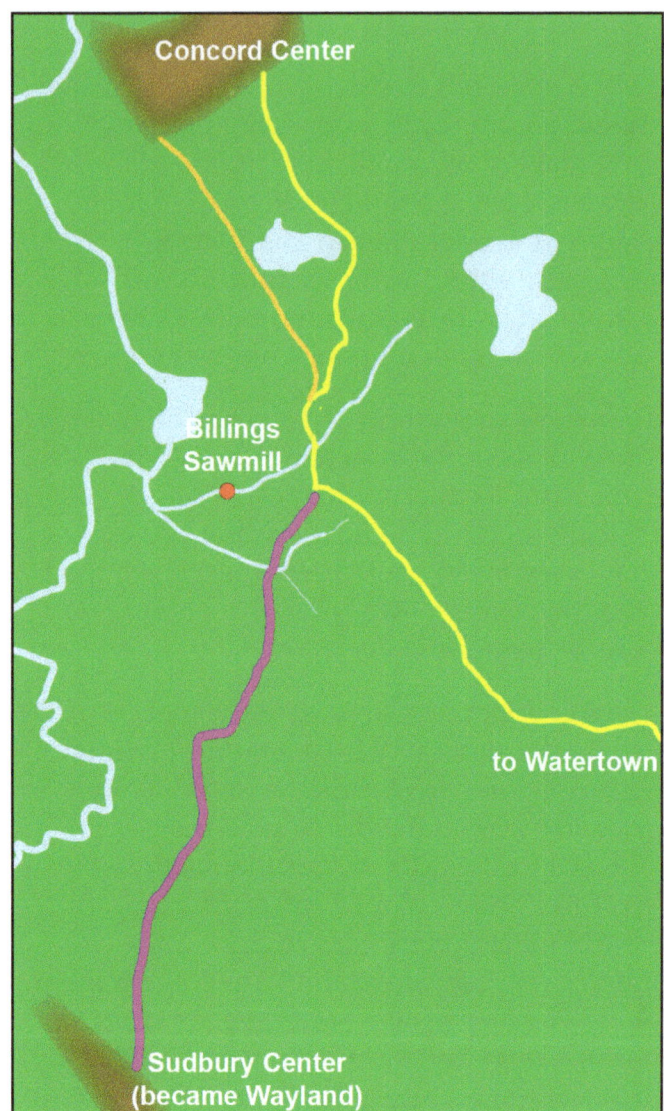

The route shown in orange ran from the south side of Concord village on what is now Fairhaven Road. The Walden Street route, shown in yellow, turned left on present Codman Road. The magenta way to Sudbury is present Route 126.

Adapted from "Tracing the Ways" by Kerry Glass, 2010.

avoided swamps. From Concord, routes to Watertown passed on both sides of Walden Pond, then joined and bent southeast through what eventually became Lincoln, to follow present-day Routes 117 and 20 to Watertown Square and the Charles River. From below the falls, goods could be moved across the estuary to and from Boston and Charlestown.

A proprietor of Concord, Nathaniel Billings (1600-1673), lived in the village, on Walden Street. By 1654, when Concord made its second division of land, Nathaniel had two sons, John (1640-1704) and Nathaniel (1649-1714). The three male Billingses received over four hundred acres astride Beaver Dam Brook and the road to Sudbury. They farmed their arable land, cut trees from their sand plains, and built a sawmill on their brook. In 1678, five years after their father's death, the sons sold the village property. Their new houses were near the sawmill and their farms, which were separated by the road that became Route 126.

With that, let's begin a tour on foot, starting at the parking lot of the Mount Misery Conservation Area.

The house at 44 Walden Street in the 19th century, called the Billings/Estabrook House. Nathaniel Billings and his sons lived here. (Photo by Alfred W. Hosmer, Courtesy Concord Free Public Library.)

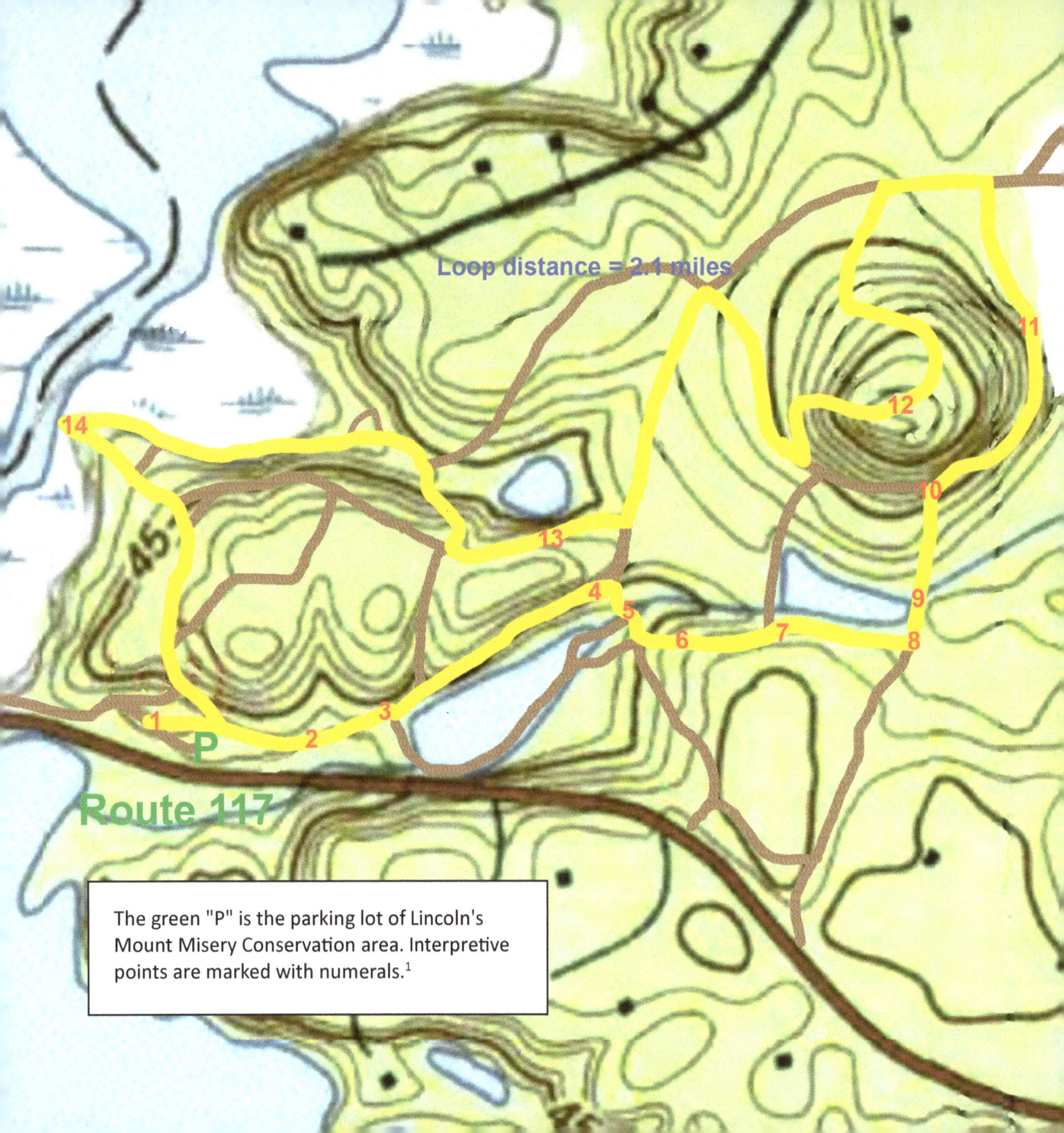

Brook, and North Branch of Halfway Brook. (Halfway Brook drains the area to the east of Beaver Dam Brook. Since Ed Farrar built his dam, around 1900, both streams flow through Farrar Pond on their ways to the Sudbury River. The point at which Halfway Brook crosses Route 126 is midway between Wayland and Concord centers.)

Point 1 - Garfield Cellar Hole

In 1788 Timothy Billings, Jr. (great-great-grandson of immigrant Nathaniel Billings) sold two and a quarter acres to Thaddeus Garfield, with water rights. We stand in front of the Garfield farmstead.

There was scant reason to extend an east-west road to the river until it was bridged, in 1760, so until then this corner of the Billings land was unoccupied. After the bridge and the road to Concord were constructed, Thaddeus Garfield apparently saw an opportunity here.

Charles Francis Adams, Jr. bought the Garfield farm in 1894, granting a life estate for "old Mr. Garfield." The house was in poor condition and was taken down after his death.

The stream that crosses Route 117 on the map at left is the same one that crosses Route 126 at Lindentree Farm. It is variously referred to as Beaver Dam Brook, Beaver Brook, Sawmill

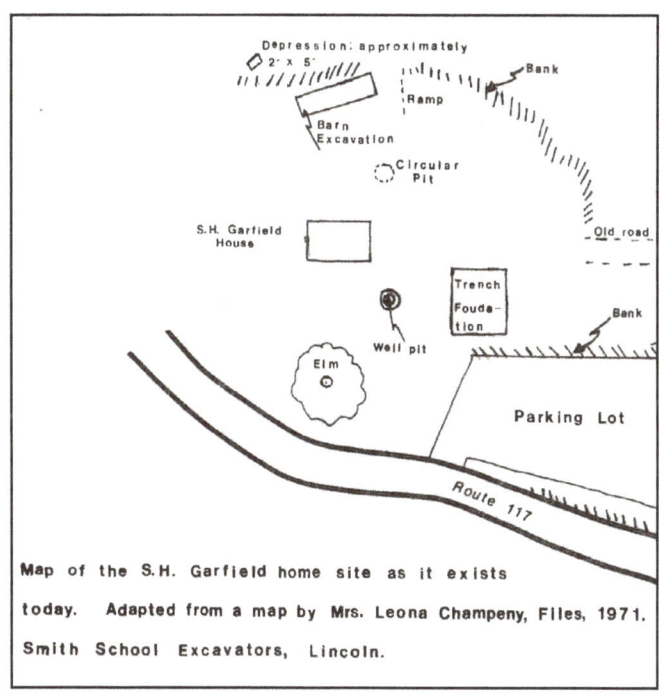

From "Springer Monograph," courtesy Lincoln Land Conservation Trust.

Along the way - Granite

Most of the parking lot boulders are granite, rock that solidified slowly, deep below Earth's surface. The gradual cooling allowed the constituent minerals to form the crystals that give granite its texture. Granite's colors vary.

Granite is the most common igneous rock found at Earth's surface. The cliffs of Fairhaven Hill are granite.

Point 2 - Garfield Aqueduct - Left of Trail

About forty yards beyond the kiosk, opposite the first boulder you come to on the right, there is (at this writing) a fallen log a few yards to the left of the trail. On the right side of the log, note the trough-shaped depression in the soil. Elizabeth Little's map (facing page) labels this long trench "aqueduct." Perhaps in its day it was lined with planks.

The source of the water thus carried to the Garfield place was a low dam that we will see from the bridge farther on. Why did Garfield want this water? Perhaps in the summer the brook's flow was exhausted irrigating the field that was where the skating pond is now, so the Garfields needed to bring water from above to for their gardens and their stock.

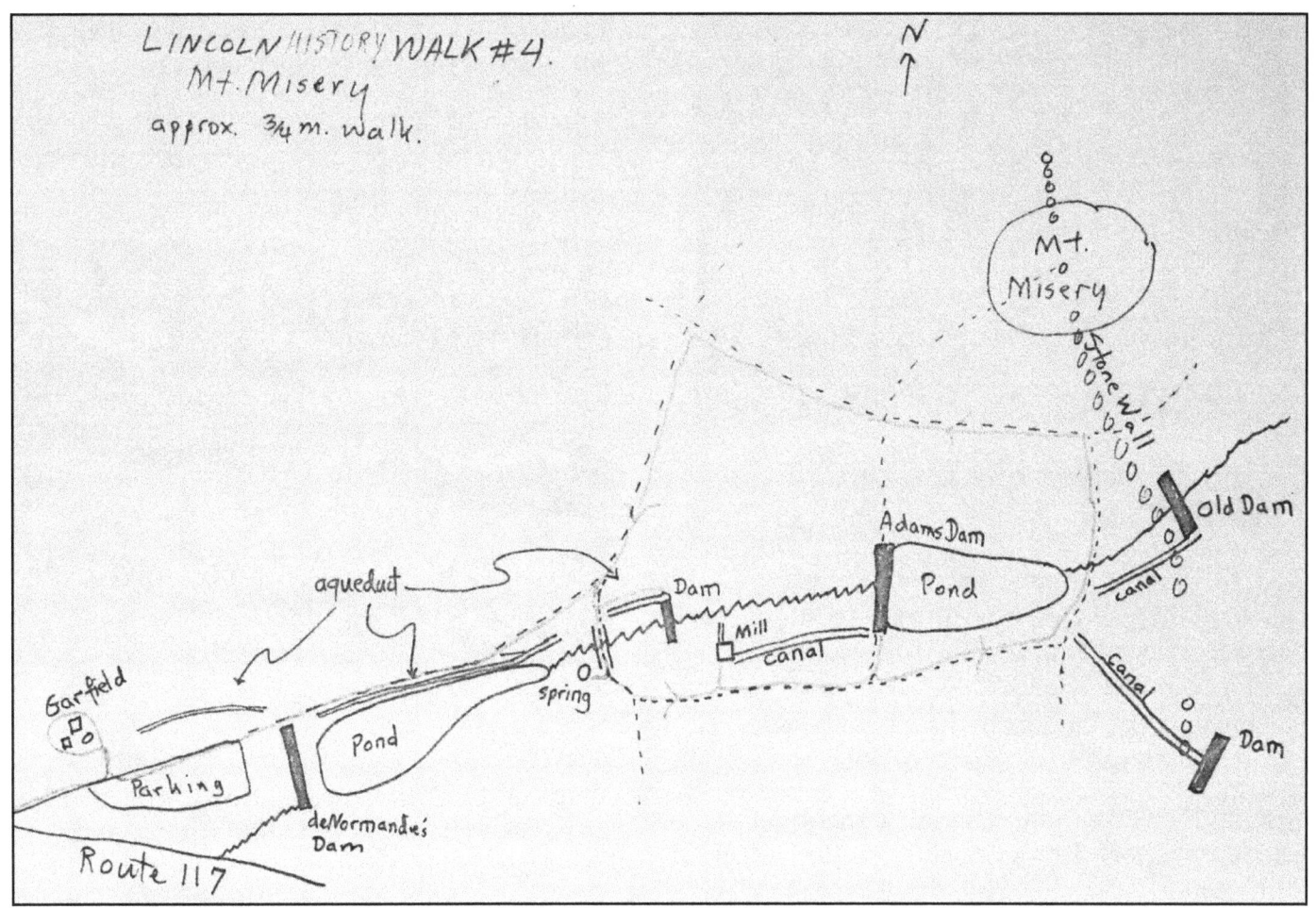

Archaeologist, physicist, and Lincoln historian Elizabeth A. Little (1937-2003) led a walk over this ground in 1971, two years after the town bought the land to conserve it. One of the resources thus preserved is the site of the Billings sawmill, shown near the center of "Betty" Little's map.

Note the location of the shallow trench she labels "aqueduct."

"Elizabeth Little Papers," Lincoln Public Library.

Point 3 - DeNormandie Dam and Skating Pond

As we walk upstream, the youngest of several dams we will see forms a pond that freezes early and attracts ice skaters. A Lincoln family named DeNormandie acquired land here from the Adams estate and other landowners in the 1940s.

James DeNormandie built this dam about 1954. Mr. DeNormandie said, in a 1981 interview, "Where the pond is now, that was an open field. … We dug a lot out of there. They used much of the dirt to rebuild new Route 117. It worked out very well, because it enabled us to build a deep pond. They had clay and heavy things to build the core of the dam. That is a good dam. It is much better than the upper one. The dam that is at the upper pond is the old dam. It is just somewhat repaired and raised a little bit. It was in poor shape and had washed out."[2]

James DeNormandie served in the Massachusetts legislature from 1955 to 1972.

He died in 1987 at the age of 80. (See page 19 for more about the DeNormandies.)

The town of Lincoln bought this and adjoining tracts of land in its first conservation purchase, in 1969.

Point 4 - Trail Intersection

The trail ahead leads to the community farm fields and to Old Concord Road, which would have been the way to the Billings house on Walden Street. We are near the location of the Billings sawmill. We take the path down to the right, which leads to a bridge just below the mill site. The Billingses probably began sawing logs into lumber about 1670. New England colonists did not use log cabins; they wanted board houses.

If the Billingses were taking lumber to market in Concord, perhaps they hauled boards to the river and floated them to town. The easiest route to the river would have been through the kettle to our northwest, then on down to the shallow bay below. Ice and snow would have reduced the effort required of their oxen.

If the lumber was to go to Concord or Sudbury by land, the hauler would certainly have wanted the flattest route available. Perhaps customers bought their boards at the mill and made their own decisions about how to transport them.

Point 5 – Bridge

Continuing our transportation speculations, the path going east from the bridge leads toward the intersection of Routes 117 and 126. If you want to go from here to Watertown or to Sudbury (which became East Sudbury in 1780, then Wayland in 1838), you start at that intersection.

Looking upstream from the bridge, you can (barely) see a low dam with a breech. That dam stored water for the Garfields, and fed their aqueduct.

Notice the care with which the rocks were fitted into the bridge abutments. There might have been a bridge here for 350 years, but these abutments are probably much younger.

On the other hand, perhaps the spring below the bridge, near the left bank, has furnished drinking water for the mill hands, and for passers-by, since early times.

Below this point, the brook flows gently downhill until it enters Farrar Pond, which was created around 1900. Before then, this brook merged with Halfway Brook (AKA Pole Brook and Otter Brook), crossed under the road to Lee's Bridge, and entered the Sudbury River.

If you could view Beaver Dam Brook from the side, at a distance, you would see its profile, which takes a steep drop in the hundred yards above this point. The opportunity to capture the energy of that falling water is why the Billings family built a sawmill here.

Point 6 - Mill Site

Our trail bears left and climbs. At its high point, look down the slope to the left. There is a depression below and to the right, where water flowing from the millpond swirled and entered the mill's sluice.

Unless it was at a sheer waterfall, a mill powered by water needed a "head-race"; a canal that brought water to where it could, by its falling weight, turn the wheel. You are at the end of the head-race. The wheel would have been in the pit, shown above, that is farther from the trail.

Colonial sawmills were usually powered by an undershot "flutter wheel" that was wider on the axle dimension than across its diameter. The wheel turned a crank that raised and lowered a "sash," a wooden frame into which a saw blade was mounted vertically. We can imagine the Billingses ordering the blade, crank, and other metal parts to be brought from England. Perhaps they built the frame of the mill while they waited for delivery.

Looking down hill to the left, we can guess that three centuries ago we would have seen an open, sunny area, with boards drying on racks.

Dependent as it was on water, this mill was probably always a seasonal operation. Perhaps the Billingses concentrated on farming during the warm months, felled trees after the harvest, dragged logs here when there was snow to skid them over, and ran their saw during the late winter and spring, when the supply of water was most reliable.

One man who probably worked here was William Fillis, who was freed from enslavement by a Billing[3] of the fourth generation. The deed is in the records of Middlesex County.

> I Nathaniel Billing of Lincoln in the County of Middlesex in the Province of the Massachusetts in New England, Yeoman, In Consideration that my Servant William Fillis has continued faithfully in my Service for many Years past and more especially that he the said William hath in my old age for Sundry years past behaved himself toward me and my Wife with Care and Tenderness do give and grant unto the said William from this Day and forward during his natural Life the Right and Freedom of Every English Subject of his Majesty King George the Third of Great Britain and as accordingly acquit and discharge him the said William Fillis from any further Service for me or mine as a servant or an Apprentice In Witness whereof I have hereunto let my Hand and Seal this twelfth Day of Jan, 1763.

The nightmare institution was real, and it was right here!

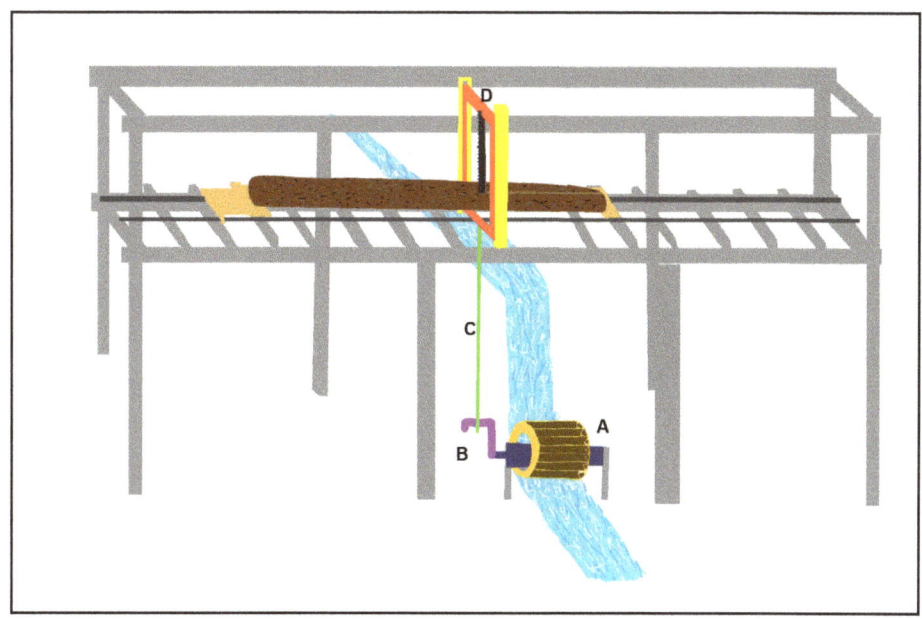

Schematic design of typical early American sawmills. Falling water turned the undershot "flutter wheel" (A), which turned the crank (B). The crank raised and lowered the "pitman" (C) which moved the sash (the frame that held the saw) (D, in red) and the blade up and down.

Not shown are the mechanisms to advance the log and to close the sluice when the saw reached the end of the log. Imagine trying to keep all this working, in the woods far from town, with the technology of the colonial period. Could they afford to inventory spare parts?

Adapted from *The Young Mill Wright and Miller's Guide* (Philadelphia, 1795) by Oliver Evans and Thomas Ellicott.

Point 7 - Mill Dam and Pond

Standing here before the Billingses dammed the brook, we would have watched it tumble down the shoulder of Mount Misery onto the softer rock below. Perhaps the original mill was built just below the near end of the dam, above the natural channel of the brook. The spillway at the far end of the dam created a new, higher channel.

A mill here would not have needed the ninety-yard headrace that carried water to the site below. Why have your mill at the lower location? Perhaps to capture energy from the few feet of additional fall the brook takes between here and there. Or perhaps because it was easier to supply that location with logs or to move lumber to the river.

When and why did the mill cease operation? Had all the trees been cut down? That could have been the case, but for a small-volume, short-season sawmill, the sandy hillsides might have produced a reasonably sustainable crop of pines.

It would have been a lot of work to build and operate the mill. In colonial times, the demand for boards, and the Billingses need for cash, must have made the effort worthwhile. But market conditions changed. The Fitchburg Railroad, built in the early 1840s, would have scotched the competitiveness of any such enterprise as the sawmill on Beaver Dam Brook—but probably it was out of operation decades earlier.

The Middlesex Canal opened in 1803. The Concord River was the highest source of water on its route. Lumber rafted down the Merrimack River from abundant supplies of timber and water power in New Hampshire crossed the Concord above the dam in North Billerica. There was no dam upstream of that one on the Concord River, and none on the Sudbury until the falls at Saxonville, in Framingham. Once the Middlesex Canal was built, lumber could have been moved by water from New Hampshire to Concord, Sudbury, and East Sudbury.

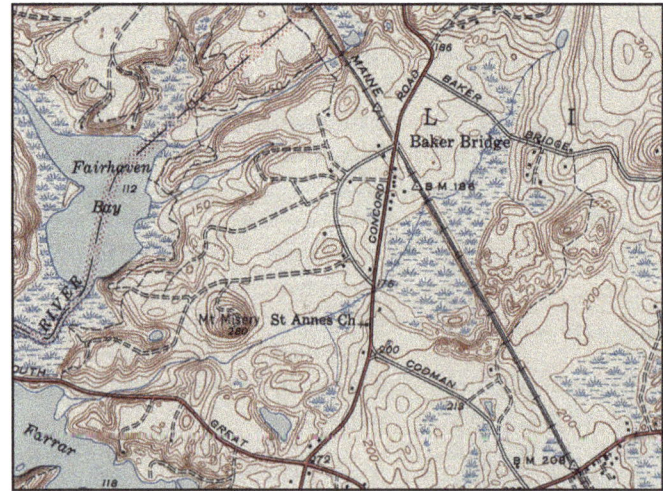

Detail from USGS Concord Quadrangle, 1943.

Along the way - Pillow and cradle

Note the humps adjacent to depressions on the forest floor to the right of the path. This is called "pillow and cradle" topography. It is created by the blow-down of large trees. Soil and stones lifted by the tree's roots falls into a pile. When the tree decays, all that remains is the bump next to a shallow hole. Pillow-and-cradle is frequent in this forest.

Probably most of the blow-downs were during the Hurricane of 1938. In a 1981 interview, Quincy Adams said, "That hurricane blew harder than any other hurricane we have ever had around here. The trees were not going down in one fast drop; they were just laid down, one after another. The road in front of our house was filled with trees."

Point 8 - Trail Intersection at Corner of Mill Pond

The trail leading off to the right climbs, at an even gradient, to Route 117, which it reaches at the top of the hill on the way to the traffic light at Route 126. This would have been a logical land route to either Watertown or Sudbury.

Just past the trail intersection a small brook seeps under the trail. Looking upstream, notice the remains of a low dam. Farmers flooded their meadows to allow fertilizing silt to settle. Or the dam might have been for cranberries. Quincy Adams recalled, "All the lowlands were partially in cranberries, and in all of the marshes along Fairhaven Bay. We use to pick them down along the bay when I was a youngster. We had a flat boat up in the barn with cranberry scoops that had been left from the time the Bakers harvested cranberries. Cranberries were a big crop around here."[4]

The brook slowly finds its way through the beaver-flooded marsh between St. Anne's Church and the community farmland and finally reaches the point just upstream of us.

Point 9 - Bridge above Mill Pond

Beaver Dam Brook drains the portion of southwestern Lincoln outlined in yellow on the map at right. Its source is at the foot of Pine Hill. The brook flows through its first pond near what is now the Thoreau Institute, and falls steadily toward Baker Bridge Road. Why did the Billingses not build their mill there instead of below Mount Misery? Probably because that point, higher in the watershed, had less water power. Also, although that location would have been nearer to the Concord market, lumber would have had to be transported by land—that site lacks access to the Sudbury River.

Beaver Dam Brook flows under Baker Bridge Road, through a big swamp, and then goes beneath Route 126. Today the stream passes unnoticeably beneath the road in a culvert. In colonial times, that soggy place would have been an obstacle on the road to Watertown and Sudbury. It was crossed by one of the bridges built and maintained by the community early in Concord's history.

Along the way - Stone wall

As you ascend the slope of Mount Misery, notice the stone wall to the right of the trail. This wall continues over the top of Mount Misery and down the other side. Intriguing! Presumably at one time this was a property boundary. The rocks comprising the wall pose a question. Notice that many of these stones have sharp corners and edges. Why aren't they as rounded as those in the same wall on the other side of the hill?

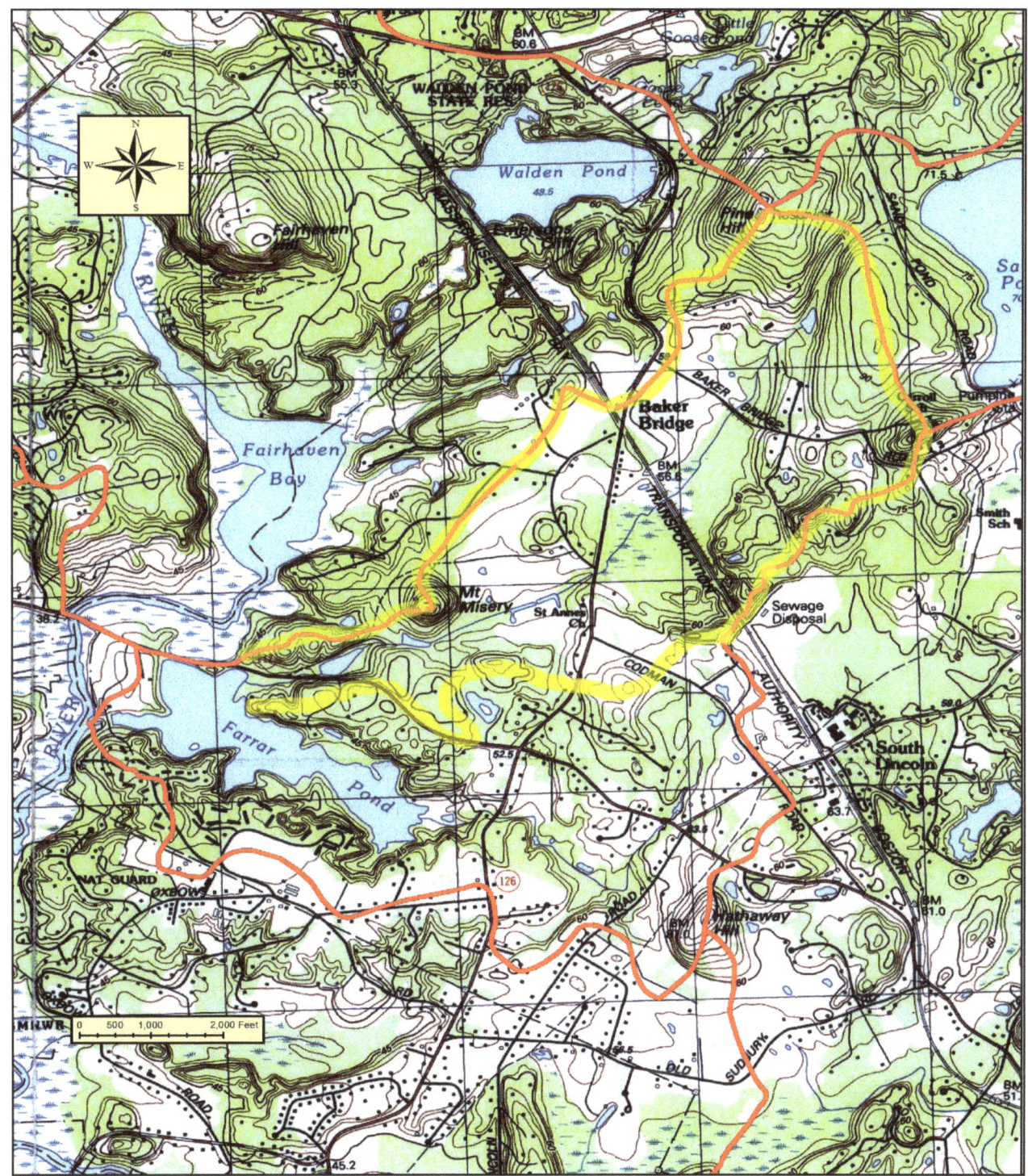

Point 10 - Below the Cliffs of Mount Misery

Many hills in eastern Massachusetts are made of loose materials: sand, gravel, silt, and clay. Other hills are high points in the bedrock. On this walk, we encounter both. The flat-topped hill rising behind the Garfield farm is a deposit of sand and gravel released as the glacier melted. This material was carried by ice-bordered streams until it settled into deltas, also called sand plains. When abutting glacial ice finally melted, steep slopes were left behind.

Mount Misery is bedrock; it preceded the glaciers. Here, a knob of rock proved more resistant to erosion than the rock that had surrounded it. In a time-frame far longer than the relatively few years going back to the ice age, weaker rock was worn away, leaving this hill.

Glaciers could not scrub away bumps of bedrock, but they did have an effect. Bedrock cracks as it reaches the pressure-free zone of the surface. Glaciers put their icy fingers into these cracks. As they flowed, they tore, leaving an asymmetrical hill, steeper on the downstream side than on the upstream. Geologists call the lower side the "lee" slope—that's what we're standing on. The gentler upstream side is called the "stoss" slope. Sand dunes often have stoss and lee formations created by the wind.

Another term for the topographical result seen here is *roche moutonnée* (or sheepback). Fairhaven Hill is another sheepback, but it is granite, whereas Mount Misery is basalt, a dark-colored, fine-grained, igneous rock.

Rocks plucked from a lee slope, if left nearby, can be expected to have sharp edges, because they have not been tumbled along by flowing ice or liquid water. That's why the wall stones look different here than on the other side of the hill.

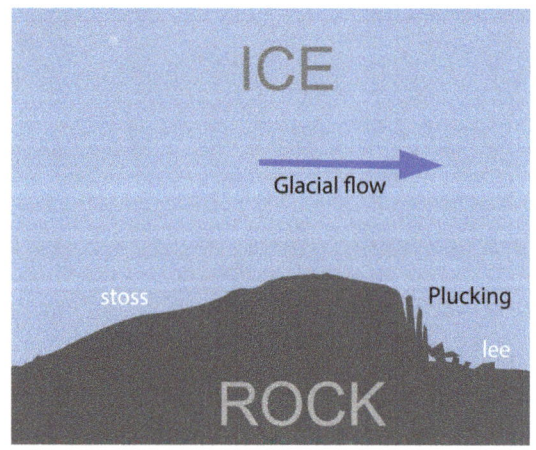

How sheepbacks form under glaciers.

How did Mount Misery get its name? Betty Little wrote:

> Mrs. Leslie Anderson, a longtime resident of the neighborhood, recently told us this story. Her mother used to tell her that two oxen, yoked together, got lost and found themselves on opposite sides of a sapling on the mountain. Too foolish, as oxen are, according to Mrs. Anderson, to back up, they were not found until after their death. Hence the name: Mount Misery.[5]

Whereas, Quincy Adams said:

> Elliot Bunker told me, and of course it came from his family, and it was a legend around town that there was a cow that fell off the mountain and broke its neck. The cow died in misery at the bottom, but whether the cow really died in misery or it was the misery of the farmer I do not know. That was the established tradition.[6]

There are Mount Miserys in many other states and countries. No one really knows how this hill got that name, but all of the stories seem to involve cattle.[7]

Do the depressions huddled against the hillside mark the sites of early structures?

Point 11 - Cellar Holes and Community Farmland

To the left of the trail is a group of shallow depressions. Their location is protected from west and north winds by Mount Misery. They are between the mill site and the fields to the east. The original Billings brothers eventually built houses nearby, on the road to Concord. Perhaps before that time they had a cabin here, and a little barn, to use when their permanent residence was still on Walden Street in Concord village. They could camp here rather than make that three-mile hike every night.

Did the Billings brothers awaken here, on the morning of April 21, 1676, to the sound of distant gunfire, as Metacom's warriors attacked Sudbury, in the last big battle of King Philip's War? Could the brothers see the smoke of burning houses? Perhaps some of the Concord men who rushed toward the fight, and perished, were their friends.

Up ahead is the main trail that connects the parking lot on Route 117 to the community farm land we can see through the trees. Lindentree Farm stretches to Old Concord Road on this side of the trail. Codman Farm uses the field north of the trail. Both operations are owned by the town and managed by skilled farmers.

Point 12 - Summit

Here our elevation is 290 feet. Toward the end of the last ice age, we would have been standing on an island rising from a huge, frigid, body of fresh water—Glacial Lake Sudbury.

Glacial lakes formed when water backed up against the face of the northward-retreating ice, flooding lowlands behind it. The level of the lake was determined by the lowest point in the surrounding ridges from which water could escape, which geologists call the spillway.

The ice front that dammed Lake Sudbury is thought to have been approximately where Route 2 crosses Concord. The lake reached eighteen miles upstream to Framingham. Its shape was irregular. At one stage an arm reached through the valley of Cochituate Brook to connect with a similar lake in the basin of the Charles. At a lower level, the spillway appears to have been at Cherry Brook on the Weston-Wayland boundary.

The flat tops of the sand plains in this area show the level of a long-lasting surface of Glacial Lake Sudbury.

Mount Misery was a destination for Henry Thoreau, when his rambles took him southeast from Concord. In his time, trees did not obstruct the view as they do now. Here are sample entries from Thoreau's journal.

> June 15, 1852 On Mt. Misery, panting with heat, looking down the river. The haze an hour ago reached to Wachusett; now it obscures it.

> August 23, 1853 Looking down the river valley now from Mt. Misery, an hour before sundown, I am struck with nothing so much as the autumnal coolness of the landscape and the predominance of shade.

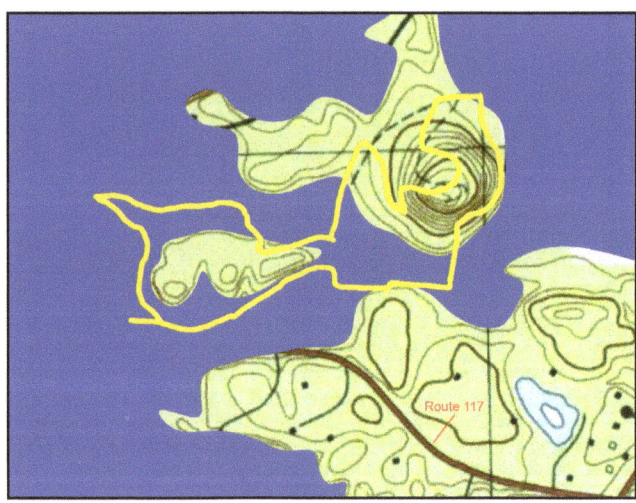

The yellow loop is the route of this walk. The blue shows Glacial Lake Sudbury when its surface was approximately 165 feet above today's sea level. The Sudbury River elevation, at Lincoln, is 110 feet, which suggests the approximate depth of the glacial lake.

In the early 1950s, Jim DeNormandie built a cabin here. His son Robert recalls:

> We spent a lot of time roaming around Mt. Misery. We spent many fun evenings in the cabin Dad built atop Mt. Misery. Dad grew hay for his Guernsey cattle in the fields between Mt. Misery and Old Concord Road.[8]

Along the way - *Stoss slope*

The stone wall to the right of the trail is a continuation of the wall we encountered on the other side of the hill, where it was built of fragments of Mount Misery's gray rock. Here, on the stoss slope, we find mostly rounded granite stones. The glacier climbed this side of the hill, deposited sand and rocks, and left a gentler slope. Plenty of trees grow here, and they all would have been uphill of the sawmill, meaning less work to move the logs.

Point 13 - Above the Kettle

As, in fits and starts, the glacier retreated, large chunks of ice were left behind to become covered with sand, gravel, and boulders. When the buried ice eventually melted, it left what is called a kettle, or kettle hole.

If the level of surrounding groundwater is higher than the bottom of the kettle, a pond is formed. The depression on our right is an example of a kettle with a very small pond. Walden, White, and Flint's Ponds are larger glacial kettles, and so is Fairhaven Bay, which the Sudbury River flows through.

Along the way - Trench from kettle pond

Along the way - Trail between ice face and shrub swamp

Back at Point 4, at the trail intersection, we saw how lumber could have been taken from the mill to the rim of the kettle. From there, it was all downhill to the river—almost. The lumber would still have to get over this low ridge. The ditch we see here might have been created to ease that passage, or maybe it is simply the result of oxen dragging boards toward the river during many mud seasons. Once the lumber was down to the swampy bay of the river, it could have been towed along the shore to the river, then rafted or boated down to Concord to be sold.

Or perhaps this ditch had some other purpose, unrelated to the mill.

The steep sand slope to the left formed when the bay to our right was a huge lobe of ice, an extension of the enormous mass that formed Fairhaven Bay. Over time the delta to our left piled up against the side of the ice, as melt-water flowed into the glacial lake. When streams enter still water, they lose the energy necessary to carry a "burden" of sand and gravel. We can see the delta taper as the stream's energy dissipated into the body of the lake, allowing sand and gravel to settle.

Point 14 - Sudbury River

The river flows from left to right. From its source in Cedar Swamp, in Westborough, near the intersection of Route 495 and the Mass Pike, the Sudbury passes between Hopkinton and Southborough, flows through Ashland and Framingham, and forms most of the boundaries of Wayland with Sudbury, and Lincoln with Concord. Fairhaven Bay is just downstream. Four and half miles from here, by canoe, the Sudbury joins the Assabet to form the Concord River.

Between the falls at Saxonville, in Framingham, and the dam at North Billerica, the Sudbury and Concord drop very little. With a gentle current and without portages, this stretch of river is a favorite of paddlers.

In 1998 the lower Sudbury, along with the connecting undammed portions of the Assabet and Concord, were federally designated as Wild and Scenic Rivers, and afforded protections in recognition of their unusual qualities, which were identified as historic and archaeological, ecologic, recreational, scenic, and the remarkable place in American literature they occupy.

Along the way - Trail back to Garfield's

When the aqueduct was dry, did Garfield stock climb this low ridge to drink from the river? When I pass this way, I like to imagine the animals walking here.

Notes

1. For information about all of Lincoln's trails, see "Trail Map of Lincoln Massachusetts" and *A Guide to Conservation Land in Lincoln*, both published by the Lincoln Land Conservation Trust.
2. Interview by Jo Springer, 1981. Lincoln Public Library Archives.
3. Over the generations, the family dropped the "s" from Billings.
4. Interview by Jo Springer, 1981. Lincoln Public Library Archives. Quincy Adams (1907-2003) was the grandson of Charles Francis Adams, Jr. (1835-1915), who was grandson of one President Adams and great-grandson of the other. From the 1890s to mid twentieth century the family had extensive land holdings between Old Concord Road, Fairhaven Bay, and Farrar Pond.
5. Elizabeth Little, papers. Lincoln Public Library Archives.
6. Interview by Jo Springer, 1981. Lincoln Public Library Archives.
7. "Misery" formerly was more like a synonym of "poverty" than it is today. Perhaps the hill's name was a humorous complaint by its yeoman owners about its extremely sandy soil and consequent uselessness for farming.
8. Personal correspondence. Robert DeNormandie also wrote: "Dad initiated a Guernsey Dairy Farm which operated from the early 30's until the mid 60's. During that time, he partnered with Floyd Verrill in Concord to found the DeNormandie & Verrill milk business that turned into the Concord Dairy. The bottling plant was at the corner of Thoreau Street and Sudbury Road in Concord. I and my brother, Phil, recall doing chores at the farm during our high school years. I helped in the morning and Phil worked in the afternoon.

    "When development began to push into Lincoln in the 50's and 60's funds became available for purchase and protection of land for purposes of conservation and maintenance of open space. At one point, Dad and Mom decided to work with the Town to access such funding to acquire the Mount Misery parcel as open space for the Town and general public. This became the cornerstone of Lincoln's conservation efforts which continue to this day. Dad was a founding member of the Rural Land Foundation which worked with local property owners to develop their properties in a way that mixed home building with conservation of key elements for future open space."

Acknowledgments

The conjectures are on me, but I had help gathering actual information. Thank you to Katie Ives, Robert DeNormandie, Jack MacLean, Don Hafner, Jen Verill, and the staffs of the Lincoln Public Library Archives and the Special Collections of the Concord Free Public Library. I appreciate the encouragement of Kim and Larry Buell, Sue and Chris Klem, and Sara Mattes. Thank you, Betsy Stokey, for editorial advice. I am grateful to those who took this walk with me—your enthusiasm led to this publication. And hats off to the Town of Lincoln's Conservation Department, which looks after this remarkable place.

References and Further Reading

Adams, John Quincy. "Transcript from an Oral Interview with John Quincy Adams Concerning Past Land Uses of Mt. Misery, Lincoln, Mass. Interview Conducted by Jo Springer, June 2, 1981." Lincoln Public Library Archives.

DeNormandie, James. "Transcript of an Oral Interview with James DeNormandie Concerning Past Land Uses of Mt. Misery Conducted by Jo Springer, June 16, 1981." Lincoln Public Library Archives.

DeNormandie, Robert. Personal correspondence.

Forman, Benno M. "Mill Sawing in Seventeenth-Century Massachusetts."*Old Time New England*. Boston, Mass: Society for the Preservation of New England Antiquities. Volume 60, Number 220 (Spring, 1970).

Glass, Kerry. "Tracing the History of Lincoln Ways", 2010. Lincoln Public Library Archives.

Goldthwait, James Walter. "The Sand Plains of Glacial Lake Sudbury." *Bulletin of the Museum of Comparative Zoology at Harvard College*, Vol. XLII. May, 1905.

Ives, Katie. "The Naming of Mt. Misery." *Alpinist*, Winter 2020.

Jorgensen, Neil. *A Guide to new England's Landscape*. The Globe Pequot Press, 1977.

Koteff, Carl. "Glacial Lakes Near Concord, Massachusetts." Geological Survey Research 1963.

Lemire, Elise. *Black Walden; Slavery and Its Aftermath in Concord, Massachusetts*. University of Pennsylvania Press, 2009.

Lincoln Historical Society. *Lincoln*, Images of America, Arcadia Publishing, 2003.

The Lincoln Land Conservation Trust. *A Guide to Conservation Land in Lincoln, Second Edition.* The Lincoln Land Conservation Trust, 2005.

Little, Elizabeth A. "Transcript from an Oral Interview with Elizabeth A. Little. Conducted by Jo Springer, June 3, 1981, Lincoln, Mass." Lincoln Public Library Archives.

McAleer, Harold. Monograph: "History of Farrar Pond." Lincoln, Massachusetts, 2000.

MacLean, John C. *A Rich Harvest; The History, Buildings, and People of Lincoln, Massachusetts.* Lincoln Historical Society, 1987.

Springer, Jo. "Historical Land Use and Land Owners of Mt. Misery, Lincoln, Massachusetts". Lincoln Land Conservation Trust, 1981.

Wessels, Tom. *Reading the Forested Landscape; A Natural History of New England*. The Countryman Press, 1997.

Wheeler, Ruth. "The Billings Family," *The Concord Journal*, December 24, 1953.

Looking across Fairhaven Bay to Fairhaven Hill.

Ron McAdow's previous non-fiction books are *The Concord, Sudbury, and Assabet Rivers: A Guide to Canoeing, Wildlife, and History*, *The Charles River: Exploring Nature and History on Foot and by Canoe*, *New England Timeline*, and, as co-author, *Into the Mountains; the Stories of New England's Most Celebrated Peaks*. His novels are *Ike* and *The Grove of Hollow Trees*. For children, he wrote and illustrated *How Dragons Got Senses*.

Ron lives and writes in Lincoln, Massachusetts, not far from Mount Misery.

PHP

Personal History Press
Lincoln, Massachusetts

Copyright 2021 Ron McAdow

www.ingramcontent.com/pod-product-compliance
Lightning Source LLC
Chambersburg PA
CBHW051306110526
44589CB00025B/2958